Scooter Fun!

written by Anne Giulieri

This is a scooter.

A scooter is fun to ride.

A scooter has a *handlebar*, a *footboard* and *wheels*.

handlebar

footboard

wheel

This scooter has 2 wheels.
But some scooters
can have 3 or 4 wheels.

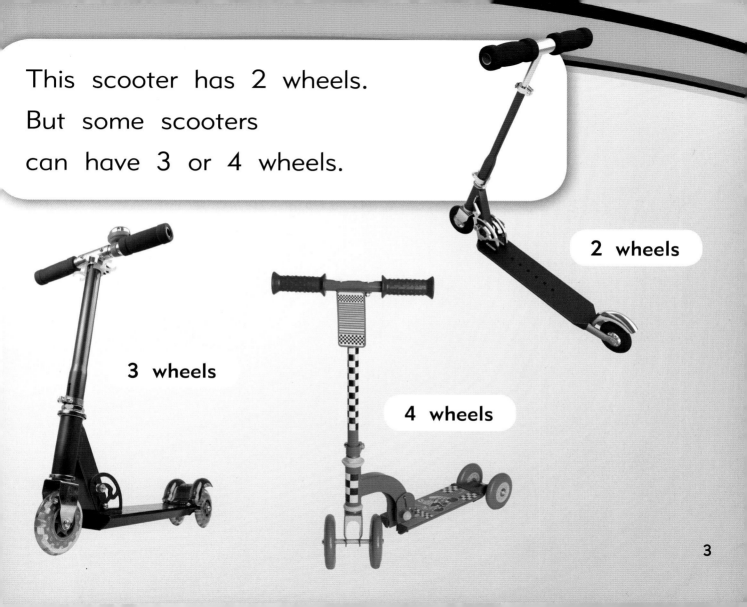

2 wheels

3 wheels

4 wheels

To ride a scooter, you need to put on a helmet.
You need to put on *knee pads* and *elbow pads*, too.
They will help you to be safe.

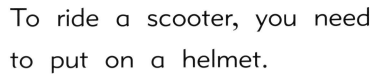

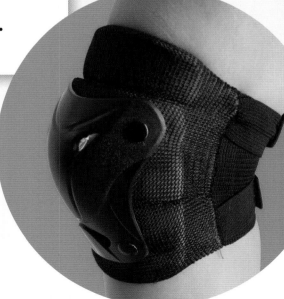

helmet

elbow pad

knee pad

5

Ships, trucks, cars and *planes* have *engines*. But bikes and scooters do not have engines. We make them *move* with our legs.

Engine

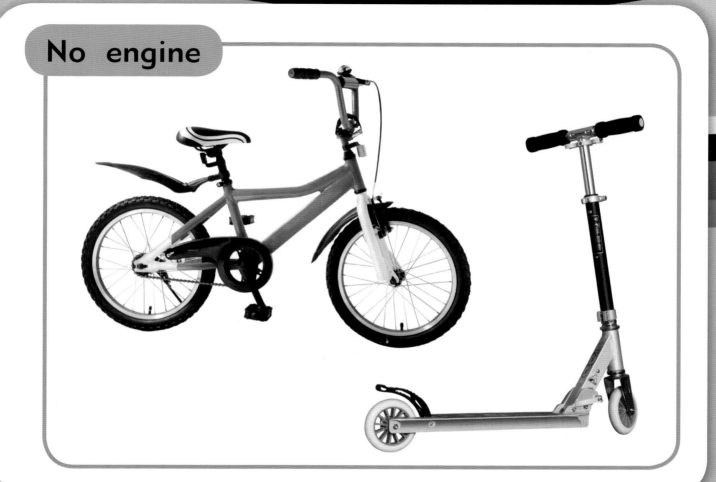

We make the *pedals* of a bike
go round and round
with our feet.
This makes a bike move.

We can also make
a scooter move
with our feet.

To ride a scooter you need to stand.
Then put your hands on the handlebars.
Now put one foot on the footboard
and one foot on the *ground*.

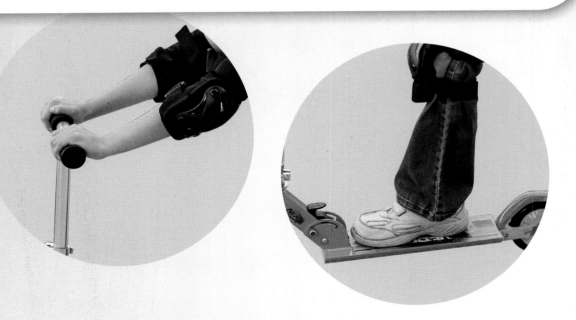

Now you are ready to move.
You have to *push* your foot
off from the ground.
This will make your scooter
start to move.
It will make it go *forwards*.

If you want
to move slowly,
push your foot
off the ground slowly.
You can also make
your scooter go
very fast, too.

You need to look where you are going
if you ride a scooter.
You need to *steer* your scooter
by moving the handlebars.
This will make the scooter
go where you want it to go.
Scooters can be lots of fun!

Picture Glossary

elbow pads

ground

pedals

wheels

engines

handlebar

planes

footboard

knee pads

push

forwards

move

steer